BEFORE
COLUMBUS

THE LEIF ERIKSSON
EXPEDITION

BEFORE COLUMBUS

THE LEIF ERIKSSON EXPEDITION

ELIZABETH CODY KIMMEL

Landmark Books®

Random House 🏠 New York

www.randomhouse.com/kids

Library of Congress Cataloging-in-Publication Data
Kimmel, Elizabeth Cody.
Before Columbus : the Leif Eriksson expedition / by Elizabeth Cody Kimmel.
p. cm. — (Landmark books)
SUMMARY: A biography of Leif Eriksson, son of Norseman Erik the Red,
who led a group of Vikings from Greenland on a voyage which ended
on the shores of North America.
ISBN 0-375-81347-0 (trade) — ISBN 0-375-91347-5 (lib. bdg.) —
ISBN 0-375-82307-7 (pbk.)
1. Leiv Eiriksson, d. ca. 1020—Juvenile literature.
2. Explorers—America—Biography—Juvenile literature.
3. Explorers—Scandinavia—Biography—Juvenile literature.
4. America—Discovery and exploration—Norse—Juvenile literature.
5. Vikings—Juvenile literature.
[1. Ericson, Leif, d. ca. 1020. 2. Explorers. 3. Vikings.
4. America—Discovery and exploration—Norse.] I. Title.
E105.L47 K56 2002 970.01'3'092—dc21 [B] 2001048294

Printed in the United States of America 10 9 8 7 6 5 4 3 2 1

First Paperback Edition July 2004

RANDOM HOUSE and colophon and LANDMARK BOOKS and colophon are
registered trademarks of Random House, Inc.

Picture credits are found on page 93.

For Bonnie, Jordan, Sarah, and David Sweet
and Holly Ellis, with love

Special acknowledgment is made to Birgitta
Wallace, Senior Archaeologist Emeritus,
Parks Canada, with grateful thanks for her
invaluable expertise and input on this book.

CONTENTS

Helluland
Baffin
Island

Greenland

Markland
Labrador

Canada

L'Anse
aux
Meadows

Vinland
Newfoundland

United States
of America

Iceland

The Homelands
Norway
Sweden

British
Isles

N

Viking **V**oyages

Erik the **R**ed ------
Leif **E**riksson ———

FOREWORD

A THOUSAND YEARS BACK THROUGH *history, almost five hundred years before Columbus made his historic voyage to the New World, another explorer crossed the Atlantic Ocean. For centuries, his name was almost forgotten, and the story of his voyage was dismissed as unlikely and unproven. Today we know more about the Viking named Leif Eriksson, who sailed west across uncharted seas and landed on the continent of North America. Only a few details of his life survive, in stories passed down from generation to generation of Scandinavians and finally written down in the thirteenth century. From these stories, called the Vinland Sagas, and from the work of archaeologists, we can now piece together enough facts to imagine what Leif's story might have been....*

PROLOGUE

THE YEAR 1000

LEIF STOOD AT THE PROW OF HIS SHIP. At his back was his crew of thirty-five Greenlanders. In the tradition of their ancestors, all men of the north, they had answered the call of the sea.

The familiar coastline of Greenland faded from view. Leif's father, Erik the Red, had been the first of his people to set foot on its shores. Now Leif wished to follow his father's example—to sail west beyond all that was known and to explore a new land.

He had little to go on. No maps. No charts. Sailors depended on landmarks and the stars to guide them to their destinations. But Leif's destination was only a myth. No such directions existed. He had only the tale told by a trader, a story Leif had begged to hear time and time again as a child. A mysterious tale of an unknown country that lay farther west than any Viking had yet ventured. A country beyond the stormy seas of what was later named the Atlantic Ocean.

Leif had dreamt of finding the unknown country of the trader's story for years. Could there *really* be land that far west? His heart told him that the land was there. And Leif was willing to do whatever it took to find it.

Pointing the bow of his ship into the waves, Leif Eriksson sailed into the unknown.

CHAPTER ONE
THE GUNNBJORN SKERRIES

THE VIKING PEOPLE HAD BEEN A POWERFUL force in the world for about two hundred years before Leif was born. They originally lived throughout Denmark, Norway, and Sweden.

The Vikings had mastered the sea in their sleek boats. They used their skills to fish and to raid villages, robbing churches and wealthy homes. Their slender, swift boats descended upon coastal villages and monasteries. Before the village people or monks knew what was happening, the Vikings swarmed upon them, swords in hand. They stole everything valuable that they could carry and were gone in a flash. In time, much of Europe feared the very sight of them. However, most Vikings spent only a small portion of their time on raids. For the rest of the year, they would remain at home, work-

This undated woodcut depicts a Viking raid led by King Olaf of Norway.

ing their farms. When they did take time off to go "a-Viking," it was as much for the experience and honor as for the treasure it might bring.

By Leif's time, the Viking raids were happening less often. Many Norsemen were more interested in finding new lands for the growing population than in seeking out new targets to pillage. Iceland had been settled over a century earlier, and Leif's father had moved there from Norway as a young man. He later became the first of his people to explore Greenland.

Leif was just eight or nine years old at the time of his father's Greenland voyage. But the memory was still clear.

The Icelandic law court, called the Althing, had made a decision. For the crime of killing two men during an argument, Leif's father was to be banished from Iceland for three years. He must leave his home and family, and he must do so at once.

Leif wondered where his father would go and how he would survive. But he did not dare ask questions. Erik's temper was as wild as the thick red hair that grew on his head. Leif did not know if it was for his hair or his temper that his father was known as Erik the Red. But he did know never to approach Erik when he was in one of his moods.

His younger brother Thorstein played happily on the earthen floor. *He does not understand what is happening,* Leif thought. *He does not know that after this night, it will be three years before we see our father again.* Tears came to Leif's eyes, and he rubbed them away.

His mother, Thjodhild, did cry. Erik remained silent. He simply packed his few belongings and ordered his servants to ready his ship.

The first printed account of the Vikings' discovery of America was a book called *Gronlandia* by Arngrímur Jónsson, published in Iceland in 1688. It featured this illustration of Erik the Red in medieval armor—an appealing but inaccurate portrayal. Erik would more likely have worn a simple iron helmet and a chain-mail tunic and carried a wooden shield.

The family took their last meal together in silence. The boiled seal meat and bread were hard for Leif to swallow because of the lump he had in his throat. After Erik had finished every last bite, he pushed his plate away and told his family where he would go—the Gunnbjorn Skerries.

Had Leif heard his father correctly? The Gunnbjorn Skerries were something from a story that had been told for many years. A man named Gunnbjorn had been sailing to Iceland when his ship was blown off course. Far in the distance, Gunnbjorn thought he saw some skerries, or rocky reefs. When he found his way back to Iceland, he spoke of what he had seen, wondering if the skerries were the outer reaches of a new land. The rocks became known as the Gunnbjorn Skerries. Nobody knew where they were or if they even existed at all.

Erik the Red told his family he felt the Skerries were there somewhere and that beyond them lay a new land. If he could not stay with his family in Iceland, what could be more honorable than to find this new country himself? Iceland was now over-crowded, and Erik wanted something more for himself and his family. Any Viking discovering a new country would have the opportunity to colonize it himself. He would become the leader of the settlers' community and would have his pick of the very best land. The move would make him a great man. Leif felt a shiver of excitement. He longed to go himself.

Leif finally found the courage to ask his father to take him along. Erik explained that Leif must stay behind. While he was away, Erik said, Leif would have to take care of the family. As the oldest son, many of the chores and responsibilities would fall on his shoulders. It would not be easy, but Leif could always turn to Tyrker for help.

Tyrker was not a Norseman. He was from the southern country, born in Germany many years ago. When he was not much older than Leif, his village had been raided by Vikings, and Tyrker had been captured and sold to Erik the Red's family as a thrall, or slave. But over the years, Tyrker had come to be almost family. The old servant often seemed like a second father to Leif. And Erik often said he would trust Tyrker with his own life. Certainly he trusted Tyrker to the same extent with his son. Leif knew there would be no more discussion. He would stay behind, as his father wished.

Leif followed his family down to the beach. When Erik was ready to depart, he said goodbye to his family. Then he walked up the gangplank and boarded his ship. The thralls on board raised the oars and dipped them into the water, and the ship glided out to sea.

Leif watched in silence until his father's ship was no longer visible. He accepted that for the time being, his duty lay at the family longhouse. But he vowed to himself that one day he would stand on the deck of a ship alongside his father, rather than waving goodbye from the beach.

And in the meantime, he could dream.

CHAPTER TWO

TO GREENLAND

TIME PASSED QUICKLY. THERE WAS PLENTY for Leif to do each day at their farm, overlooking Breida Bay. Like many Icelandic families, they lived in a simple and sturdy longhouse. It had a frame of timber and thick walls of turf to keep out the cold. There were no windows, and the only light came from the smoke hole in the roof and the fire burning in the hearth.

Leif spent hours practicing bow shooting and throwing the javelin. He worked on his horseback riding and had sword lessons with Tyrker. He developed his own strength by running, swimming, and wrestling with friends. And like all other boys of his day, he spent time learning poems to recite. There were always enough activities to keep Leif's mind off his father during the day. But at night, Leif was free to dream that he was there on the ship with Erik the Red, searching for the Gunnbjorn Skerries.

With each passing season, Leif grew taller and stronger. Tyrker teased him about how fast he was growing. Thjodhild agreed. Her son just might grow to be as tall as his father! Leif barely fit into his clothes and wondered how much more he had to grow before he became a man. Perhaps he already was one, for Erik the Red had now been gone for just over three years.

Leif knew that the day of his father's return should be very soon. Each day as he searched the beach for driftwood for the hearth, he stared out at the horizon hoping to see a ship. And one day, he did.

Leif squinted out over the ocean. He had always had unusually good eyesight. He watched for several moments, and then the sun came out from behind a cloud. Now he could see it. The broad striped sail. The fierce dragon head on the ship's prow. It was his father! Leif yelled toward the long-house. His family rushed down to join him on the beach.

The Oseberg ship, one of the best preserved Viking ships ever found, was used as a sailing vessel in the early 800s and later as a burial ship for a noblewoman. It was discovered by a Norwegian farmer in 1903 and is now on display in Oslo, Norway.

It seemed to take forever, but the ship grew larger and larger as it sailed closer. Before long, they could see Erik himself standing at the bow and waving. Leif's mother wept, just as she had when Erik had left. Leif's brother began to jump and shout. Leif wanted to shout too. He wanted to jump up and down. But he was not a little boy anymore.

He felt he ought to behave in a more grown-up way. So he stood quietly, smiling and waving.

Erik's thralls beached the ship and lowered the gangplank. Erik strode down it and waded through the ankle-deep water onto the sand. He laughed as his wife threw her arms around him and Thorstein stumbled over his feet to reach him. Leif stood to one side for a moment, and his father pushed his way over and gave him a sound clap on the back. Leif had never in all his life felt happier.

Then Erik told them the news. He had found the Gunnbjorn Skerries and, beyond them, a new land that he had named Greenland. He had explored this new land and found it completely unoccupied.

Many generations of families had remained together on Iceland, and the farms were becoming more and more crowded. Soon there would be no more room for sons and grandsons to build new longhouses and farms. Erik meant for his family to begin again in the new land. He would lead a colony of settlers there, and this time he would take his family. Leif could hardly believe his good fortune.

Erik did not waste any time. He put the word out, and within days many people responded excitedly. Erik called a meeting for all interested families and explained his plan of sailing to Greenland in two or three boats, along with plenty of food, seed, and cattle. They could have big farms there, capable of supporting large herds of cattle and sheep. All would work together to build longhouses and to

This engraving of the discovery of Greenland first appeared in an 1875 issue of *Harper's Weekly*.

farm for food. By the end of the meeting, there were plenty of families who were willing to join Erik's family and make a new start.

All that remained was to pack up and load the boats. They were crowded, but no one minded. At Erik's command, they set sail for Greenland.

At last, Leif's wish had come true. Instead of being left behind on the beach, he was setting sail with his father. But this was not a voyage of exploration. Though Leif was thrilled to be among the first to settle the new land with his father, he felt he would never really be satisfied until he and Erik undertook a new expedition themselves. Until then, Leif would concentrate on Greenland. When it finally came into view, he caught his breath.

Greenland rose out of the ocean like a dream. Leif stared at the rocky mountains, the green hills, and the icy, flat glaciers. It was more beautiful than he had imagined. What excited Leif the most was the emptiness of the place. Erik had found no one at all living there. They would be alone in taming the wild land.

They quickly settled the new country. Erik chose a steep stretch of land at the head of a twenty-mile ocean bay. Erik had his slaves cut enough sod to build himself a great hall. His hired men built the hall, which had a common sleeping and sitting area for his workers and private quarters for Erik and his family. The hall also had a kitchen and a separate work area for the women. Outside were storage huts and workshops, sheep enclosures and horse corrals, and a large cow barn. They named the new farm Brattahlid, meaning "steep

Ruins from the Brattahlid settlement can still be seen today. This photograph shows the remains of a church and a fence, with a grave marker visible between them.

meadow." Leif and Tyrker helped Erik build a sturdy and warm longhouse, with separate sleeping quarters, a dairy, and a kitchen. From the grassy and treeless land around it, Leif could look across the bay to a small row of mountains.

Greenland. Who could have imagined it was there all these years, unexplored by the Vikings? Leif wondered if even more lands lay to the west, waiting to be found.

Then one day, he heard a story that set his imagination on fire. Leif did not rest until he heard the tale directly from the original teller, an Icelandic trader named Bjarni Herjolfsson.

Though he had already told the story a hundred times, Bjarni was amused by Leif's eagerness and agreed to tell it again.

Bjarni had gone home to Iceland from Norway to discover that his father had moved to Greenland in his absence. He wanted to spend the winter with his father as he always had, so he set his ship out in the direction of Greenland. Everything had gone well for several days, until Bjarni ran into some bad weather.

His ship had sailed into a thick fog, which

enveloped it for days. He could not tell in which direction they were sailing. By the time the fog finally lifted, he told Leif, they were lost. However, in the distance they could see land. It had small hills and was thickly covered with trees. No large trees grew in Greenland, so Bjarni knew they were in the wrong place.

Some of the men had wanted to make for the new land. Why not sail in closer, go ashore, and cut down as many trees as they could carry? They would be certain to get a good price for the timber. But Bjarni refused. He explained to Leif that he had been anxious to get to Greenland before the winter came and the sea filled with ice. There was no time to lose.

They continued on a northwesterly course and twice more saw land, though not as rich as the first they'd seen. Both times, the men wanted to stop. But Bjarni again refused. Leif could not imagine how Bjarni could have turned back without exploring the new land. To think he had come so close and had turned away!

Leif hoped Bjarni might decide to look for the wooded land again. But Bjarni simply shook his

This stele, or carved stone, is an early Viking memorial from Sweden. It shows warriors sailing and riding horseback—crucial skills that Leif spent years learning.

head and told Leif he was tired of being thought of as a fool who had sailed past a treasure. He would not take to the sea again. Leif realized that if he was ever going to look for the land Bjarni had seen, he would have to go himself.

There seemed very little chance of this happening. Though he was now fourteen, Leif was still too young to undertake a trip like this. Such a voyage would require a large ship, which would take a long time to build and would cost a fortune. And Leif had nowhere near the amount required to obtain such a vessel.

There were two things, however, that Leif did have: imagination and patience. With his imagination, he was able to picture a time when he would finally have enough goods to trade for a ship of his own. And with his patience, he was able to endure the fact that it would take many years before this would happen.

In the meantime, there was much to occupy Leif. He had grown into a strong young man of sixteen and was the oldest son of an important chieftain. He had spent many years learning to handle arms and to shoot his bow, to sail and to ride on horseback. As the leading family in the Greenland settlement, Leif's relatives could now consider themselves to be among the ranks of other nobles. For Erik, there was only one logical next step for his son—he must be officially recognized by the Norwegian royalty.

It was time for Leif to visit the court of King Olaf Tryggvason.

Chapter Three

IN THE COURT OF KING OLAF

Erik arranged for Leif to have the use of a trader's ship to make the voyage to Norway. He would make for the Norwegian town of Nidaros with six other wellborn young men from Greenland. Together with their thralls, they set sail as soon as the ship had been made ready.

Leif had never sailed to Norway himself, but he had listened carefully to the directions Erik gave him, and he knew what landmarks to look for and what to expect. He enjoyed being in command. The trip took twelve days, and Leif found the trader's ship to be sturdy and swift.

They arrived in Nidaros a day earlier than expected. Leif liked the town, which had clusters of little houses and was surrounded on three sides by the river. He was excited by the new sights and

Olaf Tryggvason was king of Norway from 995 to 1000. In this illustration, he stands proudly in the prow of his ship.

smells. Though he would never admit it to his father, Leif often found Greenland boring, seeing the same landscape and people every day.

Leif particularly looked forward to meeting King Olaf. Everyone had heard stories of the King, who was said to be powerfully built and extremely handsome. He had heard a description of Olaf's fantastic dragon ship, *Long Serpent,* said to be over one hundred feet long and requiring sixty rowers!

He had also heard talk of a religion called Christianity, which Olaf had learned about when he was in England. The King had become a Christian before returning to Norway, and he wanted all of his subjects to convert to this new religion. Many people did not want to give up the old ways and gods. But they had no choice. Some were afraid because the year 1000 was almost upon them, and they whispered that the world might come to an end. But others were more afraid of making the King angry. They preferred becoming Christian to becoming the enemy of King Olaf.

Leif was not particularly interested in talk of religion. He was eager to visit the royal court and be properly introduced to the King. He did not have to wait long. Olaf heard about every ship that arrived in Nidaros, and he had been told of Leif's arrival. He knew of Leif's father, Erik the Red, and had his messengers send for the son of the Greenland chieftain.

Leif and the six Greenland noblemen went immediately to Olaf's hall, which was enormous. They were brought inside, and King Olaf himself came to greet them. Olaf was huge man with a mop of graying hair and a full blond beard. He wore a jeweled cross around his neck, and his fur cloak was fastened at his throat with a glittering brooch.

Leif presented several gifts to the King, including some narwhal teeth, a polar bear skin, and a Greenland falcon. King Olaf was pleased with his gifts and asked Leif and his men to join him for a meal. Leif immediately accepted and was pleased when he was seated in the place of honor on King Olaf's right side.

On both sides of the table, there were finely made tapestries hanging from the walls. The table was covered with a delicate linen cloth, and the back of Leif's chair was decorated with gold.

Soon the two were deep in conversation. King

The Jelling Stone was erected by King Harold Bluetooth, the first Christian king of Denmark, in memory of his parents. The engraving seen here depicts Christ on the cross.

Olaf had many questions about Greenland, and Leif answered them all thoughtfully. He described the family farm, Brattahlid, and told the story of how Erik had come to find the land. He talked about the progress the settlers had made and about their need for additional trade.

As they talked, servants brought wooden platters of food. There were apples and berries and hazelnuts. There were long loaves of bread. There were great slices of roasted bird and pork served with cooked cabbages and onions. There was even a whole pot of mustard on the table and containers of exotic spices. Leif was given some wine that tasted nothing like the sweet honey mead he was used to drinking. He ate and drank until his stomach felt as if it would burst.

King Olaf was very impressed with young Leif. As Erik had hoped, the King asked Leif to stay with him at the royal court. He would be a retainer to the King, keeping company with him, carrying out his orders, and acting as his kinsman. Leif was honored and pleased to be asked, and he agreed to stay. Though he still longed to sail west, he knew that this opportunity was too good to pass up. Being one of King Olaf's retainers would bring him honor, respect, and riches. He would stay.

Once again, his dream would have to wait.

Chapter Four

A SHIP OF HIS OWN

Leif remained at King Olaf's court for a year. He planned to return home to Greenland in the spring. Shortly before his departure, King Olaf took him aside and told Leif he had a task for him. The King wanted to send a priest to Greenland so that Leif's people could learn of Christianity and be baptized. King Olaf asked Leif to watch over the priest's progress and to help him in convincing the Greenlanders to convert. King Olaf had already personally baptized Leif. Leif knew he had no choice but to obey the King, although Greenlanders were firm followers of the old ways.

Erik was overjoyed to see Leif when he arrived home. The King had given Leif many precious gifts and tokens, and Erik was proud of what his son had accomplished. Leif had brought additional

The Borgund stave church, built around 1150, is one of the best preserved stave churches in Norway. Most early Scandinavian churches were constructed with staves, or vertical wooden planks. But because of the scarcity of wood in Greenland, Thjodhild's church, like the other buildings there, was made of stone and sod.

honor to the family by his service to the King.

Erik was less happy to see King Olaf's priest and to hear that his people were expected to change to this new religion. Leif understood his father's unhappiness. Though the King had baptized him, Leif continued with the old ways of worship and simply added the Christian god in his prayers. The Norse faith had many gods, and there was certainly room for one more. Erik, however, refused to discuss the matter.

Thjodhild, on the other hand, took a liking to the new religion right away. To Erik's displeasure, she immediately converted and began talking about building a church at Brattahlid. Leif's parents had many arguments about the subject, and it seemed they were bound to always disagree.

All winter long, Leif brought the priest from farm to farm, helping him as King Olaf had ordered. By the following spring, enough Greenlanders had agreed to convert to satisfy the King. Olaf's priest could continue the work himself. Now Leif could concentrate on his own dream.

It took Leif almost three more years to work and save what he still needed. At last, with his savings and the gifts he had received from King Olaf, Leif was wealthy enough to obtain a boat. Remembering that Bjarni had vowed never to return to the sea, he went to visit the old trader and offered to buy his boat. Bjarni immediately agreed.

The ship was a *knorr,* or merchant vessel. It was old but stately, well over sixty feet long and in excellent condition. He could not have hoped for a better vessel to sail out over the western ocean. Now he could begin to plan in earnest.

The first thing Leif did was to tell his father about his plans to find and explore the land Bjarni Herjolfsson had sighted so many years before. Would Erik agree to go along with him?

Erik the Red could well remember how it felt to see Greenland for the first time. Leif's younger brother Thorstein was almost grown now, and he could be depended on to run the estate for a time. Erik agreed to go on the journey with his son. They talked long into the night about their plans. Leif asked his father how many men they should bring along, what supplies they would need, and how long they could expect to be gone.

He spent most of each day working on the

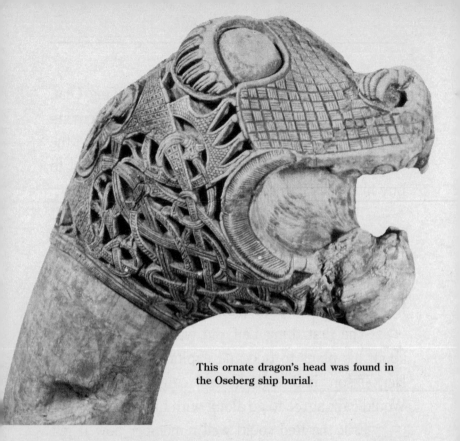

This ornate dragon's head was found in the Oseberg ship burial.

ship. The square woolen sail was made out of red and white lengths of cloth, sewn tightly together. The stripes were quite handsome, and also made the ship more visible from a distance.

On the bow of the ship was a carved dragon. Many Vikings placed these dragon heads on the front of their ships to ward off evil sea spirits. Leif loved the way that it looked, extending out from the tip of the ship to glide over the waves.

Leif went over the *knorr* inch by inch, repairing every flaw he found. He covered the overlapping oak planks with new tar to make the craft completely watertight. He had a new mast made from specially imported pine.

The supporters and tenants of Brattahlid brought large quantities of salted meat, butter, and cheese, along with *skyr* (sour milk) and oatmeal for porridge. Erik's thralls built barrels and filled them with fresh drinking water. Woolen cloth was packed for sail mending, along with plenty of heavy needles and twine. They also packed weapons and shields, including many axes and every kind of tool they thought they might need. There were smith's tongs and

A man of high rank like Leif would have carried an intricately carved ax such as this one, found in Denmark. His crew would have used plainer weapons.

anvils, knives, sickles, peat-cutting tools, nails, and sharpening stones. There was also a large iron cauldron for cooking.

Every man would have his own wooden chest in which to keep his belongings, and the chests would also serve as seats while they were at sea. Because fresh milk was very important in their diet, they also arranged to bring some sheep, a goat, and a cow.

News of Leif's upcoming voyage traveled fast, and there were many men eager to be hired for the voyage. Leif chose his thirty-five men carefully for their strength and good character. He was now twenty-two years old, a grown man, but Leif was still one of the youngest men in the group. However, the men respected their chieftain and were willing to serve Erik's son in the name of honor, adventure, and profit.

Finally, the day came when they were ready to set out. Leif stood next to Thjodhild on the beach saying goodbye. Though she did not cry, as she had when Erik had left for Greenland, Leif's mother looked strangely pale and anxious. A Viking woman expected her husband to take to the sea at one time or another. But Leif could see it was more difficult for Thjodhild to watch her oldest son do the same. Leif allowed his mother to hug and kiss him, and he gave her a confident smile.

Thorstein looked envious. There would be more trips west, Leif assured him, many more. But this first trip was his, and Thorstein must remain at home to run the estate.

It was time to go. A servant carried the last of the supplies up the gangplank. Leif looked uphill toward the farm. His father was on his way down to the beach. But as he began to come down the steep slope, Erik stumbled. He came down hard on one ankle and landed heavily in the grass. Leif rushed up the hill to his father's side.

Erik was not seriously hurt, but his ankle was very swollen. Leif offered to help his father board the ship, but Erik shook his head. This was an omen, he said. This accident was a warning to Erik the Red that he did not belong on the voyage. Tyrker must now take Erik's place on the journey as Leif's adviser. Leif knew there was no use in arguing. His heart heavy, he helped his father down the beach, then bid him farewell.

Leif boarded his ship. He ordered the gang-plank raised and the anchor pulled up. Minutes later, they were headed out to sea.

Leif checked the position of the sun, then set a course southwest. He had imagined this moment a thousand times, but always with his father standing beside him. Now he must make the trip alone.

CHAPTER FIVE

INTO A CLOUD OF ICE

GREENLAND GREW SMALLER AND SMALLER in the distance. Then the fog came suddenly, just as it had come upon Bjarni Herjolfsson so many years ago, and it was as if the land had never been there at all. Leif could not tell where the sky ended and the ocean began. He could barely see his own hand in front of his face.

He did his best to keep their course steady. Vikings depended on the sun and stars to navigate, along with landmarks. Bjarni had only a very general idea of the direction he had been heading when he saw the wooded land. He had mentioned one or two landmarks, but Leif had little hope of spotting any of them through the fog. His only choice was to keep the boat sailing in a straight line, continuing toward the southwest.

The discovery in Greenland of this fragment of a notched wooden disk has caused much speculation about Viking navigation. Some experts think it was part of a bearing dial or sun compass. Others believe it was a child's toy. No other evidence of Viking navigational instruments has been found.

The waves were rough and splashed into the open boat. Soon the men's heavy woolen cloaks were soaked all the way through. Occasionally, the fog thinned or lifted completely. Leif stared out over the ocean, looking for ice. Colliding with an iceberg could sink them. When he caught sight of a berg, Leif made a quick guess as to how close it was. When the fog settled over them again, Leif kept the iceberg in his mind's eye and steered the ship past it as surely as if he could see it.

The sun set very late that night. When it did,

the fog around them seemed to turn into a cloud of ice. The men worked in shifts to keep the ship moving. The rigging and oars were covered by a crystal layer of ice that burned the bare skin when touched. The deck was very slick, and it was almost impossible to take a step without slipping.

Leif had his own private quarters, a tent pitched on the ship, where he could sleep in relative comfort and dryness. His men, however, slept out in the open, where it was cold and wet. Each man had a heavy hide sleeping bag, but the deck was uncomfortable and space cramped.

It was frightening to be sailing blindly. Leif turned around and stared into the black water behind them. Anything could be out there. A sea worm could be rising out of the water, and he might not see it until it was too late.

Only the very foolish did not believe in the sea worm. Most everyone had heard a firsthand account of a sailor's brush with the fearsome creature. Leif himself remembered the story an old boatsman had told. He had described a frightening mass of gray coils appearing suddenly in the waves, where nothing had been a moment before.

A painting from around 1200 suggests that the sea worm was not the only mythical creature to be feared in the Viking seas. It depicts a Danish Viking ship beset by mermaids.

The old boatsman said the giant oval head rose from the water, with one huge eye in the center. The coils were covered with enormous suckers, and they reached toward the boat. The men attacked it with their axes. The scariest part of the fisherman's story was when one coil, chopped off of the sea worm by the men's axes, kept writhing even while the sailors tossed it overboard.

But Bjarni had seen no sea worms. Everyone did their best to keep that fact in mind.

On the third morning, the fog lifted again, and this time it disappeared completely. It was a great relief to see the sun again. But as the sunlight spread over the sail and rigging, the ice that had collected there began to melt. Chunks began to fall off and drop onto the deck. Leif's crew tried their best to keep out of the way, but it was hard to avoid the falling ice. By the time the sun had fully risen, quite a few of them had bumps and bruises.

Already they had made it farther west than most Vikings had ever been. They had sailed through Bjarni's fog unharmed. If the trader's experience was anything to go by, the worst was behind them.

Leif stared into the distance at something that at first seemed to be a trick of the light. But as Leif gazed intently, he saw it was no trick. He stood up and shouted to the men—land!

CHAPTER SIX

TO THE LAND OF TREES

BUT WHERE WERE THE TREES?

The land was not much more than a thick slab of rock dropped into the ocean. There were no trees, and very little plant life at all. Not even grass. There was a dark mountain in the distance.

The men looked around in silence. Leif told them not to be discouraged. Bjarni Herjolfsson had described seeing land three times. This looked like the third place Bjarni had seen, just before he found his way back to Greenland.

Although it didn't seem as if there could be anything worth exploring on the rocky ground, Leif gave the order to drop anchor. He didn't plan to spend much time ashore, but Leif was not going to make the same mistake Bjarni had so many years before. He would at least set foot on the ground.

Baffin Island, Canada, is believed to be Leif's Helluland.

Several men went along with Leif on his walk. As he had promised, he did not spend much time exploring. He stayed only long enough to give the place a name. He would call it Helluland—Flat Stone Land. Leif was as relieved as his crew to leave. They hoisted their anchor and set a course southwest, and no one looked back.

They sailed for several days, taking turns at watch, at working the rigging, and sleeping, as Leif had ordered. On the morning of the third day, Leif again spotted land in the distance. Those who were sleeping quickly awakened, and they all stared into the distance, where the smudge of land grew larger and clearer.

Here were the trees that Bjarni had described! As Leif's ship drew closer, the men could see a forest and a wide, sandy beach. Leif brought the ship as close to the beach as he could. Then he chose another group of men and waded through the water and up onto the light-colored sand.

How quiet it was. Leif signaled to his men, and they followed him to the spot where the beach gave way to trees. Leif took a deep breath, then walked into the forest. It was like entering another world. It smelled of bark and grass. There was a strange, lulling sound all around that Leif could not identify. Then he realized it was the sound of the wind rustling thousands upon thousands of fir treetops. He had lived in a treeless country for so long, Leif had forgotten what it felt like to stand in the woods.

In 1570, well after Christopher Columbus's celebrated discovery of the New World, the Stefansson map was created to prove that Northern Europeans had been to America before Columbus. Although it was based solely on information from the sagas, it helped point archaeologists toward Newfoundland in their search for evidence of a Viking presence in North America.

The men behind Leif stood in silence. Each one felt a sense of awe at being the first of their people, perhaps the first people at all, to stand in this spot.

They would call it Markland, Leif told his men. The Land of Forests.

But Bjarni had spoken of sighting land three times. The third had been Helluland, and the second had certainly been Markland. So the first place Bjarni had seen must lie farther southwest.

Some of the men did not want to leave. But Leif's mind was made up. They would find this first land of Bjarni's, and perhaps it would be the most beautiful of all.

The anchor was raised, and the men rowed the ship away from the coast, where the sail was raised and the bow pointed southwest.

Taking his place by the rudder, Leif continued the search.

CHAPTER SEVEN

THE FIRST LAND

FOR TWO DAYS AND TWO NIGHTS, THE SHIP sailed steadily on its southwesterly course. Leif had only one thing on his mind. Somewhere in the distance, perhaps less than a day's sail ahead, lay the discovery of his dreams. The first land that Bjarni had spotted, that of the rolling hills and tall trees, was the one Leif most wanted to find. This was the country, he was certain, that would be his great discovery. And he felt sure, even in the darkness of night, that it was very close.

Leif did not sleep at all during the second night. At dawn, he scanned the horizon. Off the starboard bow, he could see a dark shape. Leif pointed the bow of his ship toward it.

Slowly, the dark shape became a coastline, and bit by bit more of it came into view. By

This 1893 painting by Christian Krohg of Leif Eriksson sighting land in America is on display at the National Gallery in Oslo, Norway.

mid-morning, Leif knew they had found what they were looking for. The men shouted happily and clapped one another on the back.

Ahead of the coast itself, there lay a small, grassy island. Leif brought the ship as close as he could. He and a group of his men waded up onto the island's beach.

The island was covered in grass, and every blade of grass shimmered with dew. Tyrker put a piece of grass to his lips and drank the dew, and the others followed his example. Leif agreed with his men when they said they had never tasted water so fresh and so sweet.

They felt wonderfully refreshed when they returned to the ship. There was an inlet of ocean between the island and the coast, and Leif headed for it. There was no need to use the sail this close to shore, so some of the men lowered it, while several others took up their oars. They were moving against the current, and Leif soon realized that the tide was going out very quickly.

They took the ship in as close to shore as possible and let it settle in the sand as the seawater drained out of the inlet all around them. There was no need to be concerned about getting stuck, however. Any tide that went out would sooner or later come back in again. Until the waters rose, the ship could sit quite safely in the sandy shallows.

The anchor was secured ashore with the line running back to the boat so that the boat would not float away when the tide returned. The men waded through the shallow water toward the beach.

The inlet of ocean was met at the shoreline by

Although the winged helmets are historically inaccurate, this 19th-century engraving does a good job of conveying the bewildered excitement Leif and his men must have felt on first stepping foot in a new land.

the wide mouth of a river. Leif chose several men to join him in a walk upriver. Others would stay behind to explore the coastline, and a third group would watch their boat. With Leif in the lead, the small party of men moved forward, walking along the banks of the river where the forest began.

Some of the trees in the distance were huge. What treasure this timber could be to the Greenlanders! And who knew what else they might find of value here?

The air smelled of bark, earth, and river water. The men walked in silence, single file behind Leif. When he stopped for a moment and stood staring at the river, they all stopped too. Leif pointed into the water.

Tyrker saw it first. He had always been an enthusiastic fisherman and knew a salmon from any distance. The fish was big and fat. Now that they were looking, the men could see quite a few salmon swimming along in the river.

These were fine fish, Tyrker told Leif. Anyone coming to this place would have no need to worry about food and water. The river would provide both. Leif nodded thoughtfully.

A sound from the brush startled them. Leif whirled about in time to see two deer bounding off. He smiled. They had been ashore less than an hour and already had found sources of meat, fish, and fresh water. Leif told his men he wanted to get back to the beach and begin unloading some supplies from the boat.

They regrouped by the water, and Leif gave

the order to start moving their supplies onto the beach. The men gathered around him expectantly. Everyone had a question. Did the land look promising? What had Leif seen in the woods? Were they unloading their gear because Leif meant them to camp here for the night?

More than the night, Leif told them. They would stay the winter.

CHAPTER EIGHT
MAKING CAMP

Leif chose the site for their camp carefully. He picked an open grassy spot on the northern coast of the land.

By now, Leif had seen enough to convince him that he had discovered a rich country that would be perfect for starting a new Viking colony. Therefore he planned to make a base camp that would last for years and would have room to grow larger. They would start by building themselves a home.

First, enough sod was cut and collected to make thick walls and a roof for a large hall. The sod, or chunks of earth and grass, was packed around a sturdy wooden frame. Large trees were cut down to provide timber for the frame and additional wood for support beams and posts. The branches were saved for the roof, which would also be covered with thick layers of sod. What timber was left over after the beams and posts had been cut would be used for benches, tables, and wall paneling.

In addition to the hall, they built a longhouse for the crew, a small house for some of the workers, and huts for the thralls. They would not build a furnace unless it became absolutely necessary to make

Visitors can see these reconstructed longhouses at L'Anse aux Meadows National Historic Site in Newfoundland, Canada, where evidence of a Norse settlement has been found.

nails for ship repairs. There were several places where bog iron ore, a mineral used to make iron, could be collected. But they had no skilled smith with them, and Leif hoped a furnace would not be needed.

When the building work was completed and their immediate surroundings explored, Leif chose a group of men to accompany him in the *knorr.* They would explore more land and coastline to the south. After several days' sail, they found a good campsite. They came ashore and set up their tents in a forested area of massive fir trees. Leif divided the men into two groups and took his own to collect timber.

One night, Leif returned to the tents with his party and waited for the second group of his men to arrive. When he saw them approaching, he noticed at once that Tyrker was no longer with them.

The men could not explain what had happened to Tyrker. One minute the old man had been with them, and the next he was gone. No one had seen or heard anything unusual. They had gone back over their path calling Tyrker's name, but there was no trace of him.

Leif could barely control his anger. How could

Victor R. Lambdin's illustration of Tyrker pointing excitedly into the woods was printed in the 1902 book *Viking Tales*.

they have simply lost sight of Tyrker? Leif relied on Tyrker for guidance and advice. If any harm had come to the old man, Leif would never forgive himself.

He began to organize a search party, although it was quickly growing dark. But before they could set out, Leif saw a movement in the trees. Was it an animal or a human? All at once, a familiar figure emerged from the forest. It was Tyrker! Leif shouted, and the old German ran to meet him.

Tyrker was smiling broadly and talking excitedly in his strange German language, a tongue that no one but Tyrker understood. Leif calmed him down and told him to speak in Norse, the Scandinavian language they all spoke.

He had been walking behind the other men, Tyrker explained, when he saw something through the trees. He thought he had called out to the men ahead of him, but perhaps in his excitement he had forgotten.

He went toward the thing that had caught his eye and, to his amazement, discovered it was a grapevine. Getting down on his hands and knees, Tyrker had run his hand along the plant and followed its growth. Soon he had a handful of purple wild grapes. He was still carrying some in his hands, and he gave them to Leif to eat.

Leif was delighted. The finding of grapes would add to their honor. Not just any man could produce his own supply of wine. If Leif returned to Greenland with whole barrels of it, it would do even more for his reputation as a powerful and wealthy leader.

The next morning, Leif followed Tyrker back to the spot where he had first found the grapes. Leif was ready to give the land a name. He would call the entire country Vinland—Land of Grapes.

CHAPTER NINE

A WINTER FEAST

WHEN LEIF AND HIS MEN HAD FIRST arrived in Vinland, the sun had risen early every morning and shone straight through the day. They had spent several summer months at the little southern camp, exploring as much of the rich land as possible. They gathered grapes and butternuts, and cut lumber.

But when the days began to grow shorter with fall's approach, they packed up all they had collected and returned to their permanent camp in their northern grassy cove. Now they would have to spend more hours inside the houses. Though the workers and thralls had many chores to perform, Leif did not want his crew to become bored.

He decided they would have a feast. His men had collected a good store of deer meat and game

Leif and his men celebrate the discovery of Vinland in this undated woodcut. Again, the men would have worn plain iron helmets or leather caps, not helmets with wings or horns.

birds, and they had fished plenty of fat salmon from the river. There were also plenty of butternuts and grapes that they had brought from the summer camp and plenty of firewood for the hearth. Nothing was lacking for a fine, rowdy feast.

The thralls prepared the meat, skinning the animals and seasoning and roasting the flesh. The hearth fire was loaded with wood until it burned as bright as the sun. After hours of preparation and cooking, it was time to begin feasting.

The men gathered at the long table and piled their plates high with the delicious-smelling food. At long last, it was time to eat! The hall was full of the sounds of men chewing and making noises of satisfaction. Every man loaded and reloaded his plate until finally each man had eaten his fill. Leif leaned back in his chair and rubbed his hand over his bulging stomach. Now it was time for the storytelling to begin.

Every Viking man, woman, and child knew the stories. They were passed down from generation to generation around hearth fires and at feasts much like the one Leif and his men had in their Vinland longhouse. It was difficult to say which the men

This representation of Thor, the god of thunder, dates from the 9th century.

were more excited about—the eating and drinking or the hours of storytelling that followed.

Who would begin the storytelling, and what legend would be told? It was a cold night and perhaps a good time to hear the story of Ymir the frost giant, whose body had been used to form the earth.

Or maybe as they sat warmly by the fire, they would hear the story of Thor, who thundered across the sky in his chariot, pulled by his goats, Toothgrinder and Toothgnasher.

Tyrker was the oldest man among them and the best storyteller. It was to him that the honor of the first story fell. Tyrker chose a story that had always been Leif's favorite. It was the story of the hammer of Thor and what happened when someone dared to steal it. Leif and his men, their stomachs full of food and drink, made themselves comfortable around the roaring fire. Tyrker rose and began the tale.

Amulets of Thor's hammer have been found in many Viking burial sites. This one is on display at the Liverpool Museum in England.

Thor was the god of thunder and the oldest son of Odin, king of all gods. Thor was powerfully built, with rippling muscles and a flowing red beard. He had many magical weapons, but none so mighty as his hammer, which was called Mjollnir.

When thrown, Mjollnir had the magical property of always hitting its target. Thor used his hammer in his battles against his sworn enemies, the frost giants. Once it had struck the lethal blow, the hammer always returned to Thor's hand.

One day, Thor's hammer was stolen by a giant who wished to marry Freyja, the goddess of love and beauty. An angry Thor disguised himself in a bridal gown and sneaked into the giant's wedding feast pretending to be Freyja. Before anyone had time to react, Thor found his hammer and struck the giant down.

Leif had heard this story many times, and with each telling the events happened a little differently. But no matter how the story was told, the idea of mighty Thor dressed in the flowing bridal gown of the goddess of love always made Leif laugh.

This was perhaps their happiest night since arriving in Vinland. Leif hoped that after they had returned to Greenland, the memory of this night, with all its storytelling and companionship, would burn as brightly as the hearth fire. Perhaps one day, others would sit around a fire like this one and tell the story of Leif Eriksson and his men and their discovery of Vinland.

CHAPTER TEN
HOMEWARD

When the days grew longer and frost no longer covered the meadow, Leif told his men it was time to return home. They had collected a good deal of timber and hides. They had made several barrels of wine. And they had stories to tell, of a wondrous country large and generous enough to nourish a new generation of Vikings. Their return to Greenland would be an honorable one.

There were many things to get done. Before they could pack their cargo, the ship had to be prepared for the journey. It had spent the winter high and dry on the beach, with the sail covering the deck. Leif was glad to see that his ship had weathered the cold season well. Very few repairs were required. Even the sail looked almost as good as new.

Now they could gather up their belongings and cargo and stow them for the voyage. It would be a tight fit, and the timber would weigh them down. But the wood and wine would make them wealthy and would be proof to everyone that Leif's Vinland was a land of riches.

Though he missed his family, Leif's heart was heavy as he walked up the gangplank and onto his ship. Vinland was entirely his own, but now he would leave it behind for a time. It might be a year or more before he could return to Vinland again.

Feeling a mixture of pride and sadness, Leif gave the order to raise the gangplank and anchor. The rowers took up their oars and dipped them into the waves. When they were some distance from the shore, the sail was raised. A strong breeze blew from the land, and the sail filled with the wind. It was as if Vinland was giving them one final gift— a blast of air to get them under way.

Tyrker and several of the other men kept their eyes on Vinland as it grew smaller and smaller. Others fixed their gaze ahead, where Greenland lay. Now that Leif knew their course, the journey seemed to go much faster. They came to Markland

and then to Helluland. The next landmass they would come to should be Greenland itself.

Their journey was close to an end. But they were not safely home yet. Scanning the skies, Leif watched as iron-gray storm clouds gathered. The waves were growing larger and larger, and the ship pitched and rolled over them. Whitecaps appeared all around them, frothy and churning. The air grew

The American poet Henry Wadsworth Longfellow (1807–1882) wrote many poems about the Vikings and Norse mythology. This Viking ship on a stormy sea is an illustration from his collection *Tales of a Wayside Inn.*

thick with sea spray, which the wind whipped into the men's faces. In the darkening green-gray light, it was difficult to see anything at all.

There was no hope of navigating through such a squall. Leif simply tried to keep his ship from capsizing and prevent the wind from ripping his sail to shreds. All else was in the hands of Njord and Aegir, gods of the sea.

Above the roar of the wind, Leif could hear Tyrker shouting and pointing. Leif leaned forward and squinted in the direction Tyrker pointed. Around him, he heard the frightened cries of his men. Something was rushing toward them. Leif could just make out the flash of white ahead.

He got a tight grip on the rudder and grasped the side of the boat with his free hand, shouting out to his men to brace themselves.

Then it was upon them, a huge wave that slammed into their ship with the force of Thor's hammer. They were neither sailing nor sinking but were somewhere between the two. Trapped in a wall of green-gray water.

CHAPTER ELEVEN

RESCUE!

As SUDDENLY AS IT HAD STRUCK THEM, the wave passed by. Water rushed over the deck, but they were afloat, and whole. Leif took a quick count and was relieved to see that all of his men were still there.

The great wave seemed to have been the last show of force from the storm. Now the sky was beginning to lighten. The wind dropped off sharply. Tyrker made his way to the stern of the ship and gave Leif a clap on the back. It was good sailing, he told Leif, but they were lucky too that Aegir had let them pass.

The sun came out, and when Leif's eyes adjusted to the bright light, he was able to see what no one else had yet noticed. Ahead, distant but unmistakable, lay the coast and ice-capped moun-

tains of Greenland. Aegir had chased them into
their own backyard! In a matter of hours, they
would be home.

A reef then caught Leif's eye. There was
something on it. Leif realized a ship had gone down
nearby and the survivors were huddled on the reef
as the waves crashed around them.

Leif set a course straight for them and
brought the ship as close as he dared. Then he lowered a rowboat into the water and seated himself in
it, and within minutes he had reached the group of
castaways. There were ten or fifteen of them, shiv-
ering and overjoyed to see Leif. He brought several
at a time back to the ship. Tyrker helped them
aboard and gave them dry cloaks. In under an hour,
the whole group was safely aboard, and once again
they were headed for Greenland.

The leader of the group was a wealthy trader
named Thori. His ship had been caught in the same
storm that Leif had sailed through. But the trader's
ship had sunk. Thori and some of his men were
able to climb onto the reef. Thori had even managed
to save his treasure.

Thori showed it to Leif—a box of gold and

These Viking brooches, found in York, England, are examples of the kind of treasure Thori might have given Leif for rescuing him.

silver jewelry. The treasure now belonged to Leif, Thori told him, as a reward for saving his life. Leif was surprised and grateful for Thori's generosity, and he thanked the trader. Leif told his crew he would divide the treasure equally among his men, as they had all taken an equal share of risk in joining up with him. The men could not believe this stroke of good fortune. One of them began calling their leader Leif the Lucky.

As the *knorr* sailed up the twenty-mile length of Erik's Fjord, the bay that led to Brattahlid, Leif's heart swelled with happiness at the familiar landscape. The land had never looked so beautiful.

A single servant was standing near Brattahlid's landing place. The servant hesitated a moment, then ran up the steep hillside toward the farm. By the time Leif's ship was close enough to drop anchor and lower the gangplank, his family had spilled out of the hall and were making their way down to the dock. Leif spotted Erik immediately, his hair as fiery as ever, standing a good head taller than anyone else on the beach.

Leif walked down the gangplank and into the arms of his mother. His brother peppered him with questions. Behind them stood Erik the Red, looking pleased and proud. As soon as he could, Leif broke away from his mother and made his way to his father. It was there, Leif told Erik. Just as Bjarni said. He led Erik up the gangplank and showed him the lumber, the barrels of wine, and the box of gold and silver jewelry that Thori had given him.

Thorstein followed his older brother onto the ship, exclaiming at the rich cargo. Tyrker organized the unloading of the cargo as Leif and his family returned to Erik's hall.

Erik announced that they would feast that very evening to welcome Leif home. All of Leif's men, and Thori's too, would be welcome. Word was already spreading of Leif the Lucky's triumphant return. Neighbors and kinsmen would soon be arriving to join in the celebration and hear the stories of Leif's discoveries.

By nightfall, the hearth fire roared and the hall was filled with the smell of mead and roasting meat. The benches were crowded with people, and the air was thick with the sounds of voices raised in song and laughter. Leif sat at the head table in the position of honor, to his father's right. He ate and drank all he could, and still more food and drink was placed before him.

Finally, Leif stood up and took his place by the hearth fire in the center of the room. Everyone quickly fell silent. Looking around at the eager faces, Leif remembered how excited he felt when he first listened to Erik tell the story of discovering

Greenland. Leif took a deep breath and began to tell his own story for the very first time.

It began with a tale of a trader named Bjarni, who was blown off course and glimpsed a mysterious land in the distance. It continued with a boy named Leif, who heard of this land and began to dream of one day finding it. It followed Leif west to the wooded land of rivers and salmon. It told of Tyrker's discovery and of how the land got its name.

It was the story of Leif the Lucky, Viking explorer, and it would be repeated and passed down throughout the generations. A thousand years later, the story is still being told.

And people are still listening.

AFTERWORD

FOR MANY YEARS, IT WAS TAUGHT THAT Christopher Columbus discovered America in 1492. Now we realize that the truth of discovery is not so simple. Though stories were told of Europeans such as Leif reaching the continent of North America before Columbus, no proof could be found. But in 1960, archaeologists found the ruins of an old settlement in L'Anse aux Meadows, Newfoundland. They studied the ruins and were finally able to prove that it was a Norse camp about one thousand years old. Many feel that these ruins may be the remains of Leif's Vinland settlement.

Did our understanding of history change after this finding? If the stories of Leif Eriksson's settlement in North America are true, then how can Columbus be called the discoverer of the continent?

A spindle whorl, a bone needle, and a whetstone were all Norse artifacts uncovered at L'Anse aux Meadows in Newfoundland, Canada.

Some scholars say that if Leif found his way across the sea, others before him may also have. But since no proof has been found yet, whether there were earlier explorers still remains a mystery.

Then there are Native Americans. They had been living on the continent for many thousands of years at the time of Leif's arrival. The real discoverers of America must certainly have been the ancestors of these "Indians," as Columbus called them.

The reality is that the New World of North America was discovered time and again by many different peoples throughout the course of history. Some of them left evidence of their presence. Most did not. The history of North America is always a work in progress. With each new discovery that is made, another chapter must be added.

When the people we now call Native Americans came to the continent, the age of the New World truly began. Thousands of years later, when Leif Eriksson and his companions set out from Greenland, a new chapter in the history of the American continent was written.

It was the custom of the Vikings to pass down their history, laws, and religion by spoken description. For hundreds of years, they did not record most of these things in writing. Leif's story was passed down by storytellers from generation to generation. Eventually, some of his story was written down in the Vinland Sagas in the thirteenth century.

Even the sagas do not agree on the details of Erik's and Leif's voyages. Most of the story of Leif's trip is found in the Greenlanders' Saga. Like all of the Scandinavian sagas, it was originally an oral

This manuscript page from the Greenlanders' Saga dates from the 14th century.

history told by one generation to the next. Details were probably changed or left out along the way.

Leif almost certainly intended to return to Vinland himself, but when Erik died, Leif took over as chieftain and had to remain in Greenland. The sagas go on to tell us about more Viking expeditions to Vinland, including trips by Leif's brother, Thorstein, and his sister, Freydis. The last voyage included was that of Thorfinn Karlsefni, who began to realize Leif's dream by starting a settlement in Vinland. But trouble with the Native Americans led Thorfinn to believe there could be no peaceful Viking settlement in Vinland. He returned, along with the surviving members of his colony, to Greenland. Here the Norse chapter of North American history comes to an end.

And five hundred years later, Columbus set sail and a new age of discovery began.

AUTHOR'S NOTE

IN RESEARCHING AND WRITING LEIF'S story, I had very few historical facts to go on. The Greenlanders' Saga gave me the bare bones of Leif's journey, but the saga itself is only a written version of an expedition that happened two hundred years earlier. I chose to use many of the saga's details as facts. As to specific dates and ages, there are only approximations.

The Vinland Sagas tell us that Leif and his family lived in Iceland when Erik the Red was banished for the crime of murder. They describe Erik's discovery of Greenland and his founding of the settlement there.

The sagas go on to relate Bjarni Herjolfsson's accidental sighting of North America and his decision to turn back to Greenland. They tell of Leif's visit with King Olaf and his orders to bring Christianity to the new settlement. They also say that Leif bought Bjarni's ship and decided to take thirty-five men in search of the unknown land. They include the accident that led Erik to decide not to go with Leif on his voyage. The sagas also confirm that Tyrker, described as Leif's "foster father," joined the expedition.

The sightings of Helluland, Markland, and Vinland, the building of Leif's camp, and the plentiful trees and salmon to the south are all described in the sagas. So is the story of how Tyrker became separated from the other men when he discovered the grapes. The sagas are also the source of the shipwreck-rescue incident that led Leif to be known as Leif the Lucky.

There are many details to be found in the sagas, but many more are missing. To fill in some of the blanks, I turned to works of history and archaeology and to reference books.

Though there is no specific information about Leif's family's farm in Iceland or his *knorr* or the way his family lived, historians and archaeologists have provided plenty of facts about that time period. From those facts, I was able to reconstruct what Leif's childhood longhouse might have looked like, the activities he might have enjoyed in Iceland and Greenland, what he would have worn and eaten, and so on. From articles by historians who have studied the sagas, I reconstructed Leif's voyage to North America as it might reasonably have happened given the known facts.

The archaeologists Helge and Anne Stine Ingstad, who first discovered the Viking ruins at L'Anse aux Meadows, were able to tell the world what the site originally looked like. Through reading about their work, I was able to visualize how Leif's Vinland camp might have appeared.

Also of great importance was the assistance of Birgitta Wallace of Parks Canada, an archaeologist who was part of the original team excavating L'Anse aux Meadows. She provided me with an enormous amount of information about Viking life and about Leif's camp and exploration of Vinland in particular.

For the rest—what people were thinking and why they might have done the things they did—I used my imagination. For example, if I had been a boy watching my father leave in search of the Gunnbjorn Skerries, I would have been frustrated and worried. I would have longed to be included in the voyage, and I would have vowed to one day head out on such an expedition. So the Leif I wrote about experienced those things.

There are many blank pages in the chapters of history. Some of them can be filled in only through guesswork. History is a living work, constantly being revised as new archaeological discoveries are made and as we come to a new understanding of the past that has formed us.

No doubt, as the future unfolds, we will learn even more about our past, our New World, and ourselves.

Suggestions

FOR FURTHER READING

Clare, John D., ed. *The Vikings*. San Diego: Harcourt Brace & Company, 1992.

Cohat, Yves. *The Vikings: Lords of the Seas*. New York: Harry N. Abrams, 1992.

Corbishley, Mike. *The Vikings at a Glance*. New York: Simon & Schuster Young Books, 1997.

Evans, Cheryl, and Anne Millard, eds. *The Usborne Book of Greek and Norse Legends*. New York: Usborne Publishing, 1987.

Fitzhugh, William W., and Elisabeth I. Ward, eds. *Vikings: The North Atlantic Saga*. Washington and London: Smithsonian Institution Press, 2000.

Wright, Rachel, ed. *The Viking News: Treasure Seekers!* Cambridge: Candlewick Press, 2001.

BIBLIOGRAPHY

Almgren, Bertil. *The Viking*. London: Senate Publishing, 1999.

Anderson, J.R.L. *Vinland Voyage*. London: Eyre & Spottiswoode, 1967.

Benchley, Nathaniel. *Beyond the Mists: A Novel*. New York: Harper & Row, 1975.

Brondsted, Johannes. *The Vikings*. New York: Penguin, 1980.

Clare, John D., ed. *The Vikings*. San Diego: Harcourt Brace & Company, 1992.

Cohat, Yves. *The Vikings: Lords of the Seas*. New York: Harry N. Abrams, 1992.

Corbishley, Mike. *The Vikings at a Glance*. New York: Simon & Schuster Young Books, 1997.

Evans, Cheryl, and Anne Millard, eds. *The Usborne Book of Greek and Norse Legends*. New York: Usborne Publishing, 1987.

Fitzhugh, William W., and Elisabeth I. Ward, eds. *Vikings: The North Atlantic Saga*. Washington and London: Smithsonian Institution Press, 2000.

Graham-Campbell, James, and Dafydd Kidd. *The Vikings*. New York: William Morrow, 1980.

Grant, Matthew G. *Leif Ericson: Explorer of Vinland*. Chicago: Children's Press, 1974.

Holand, Hjalmar. *Explorations in America Before Columbus*. New York: Twayne Publishers, 1956.

Jones, Gwyn. *A History of the Vikings*. New York: Oxford University Press, 2001.

Thorsson, Örnólfur, ed. *The Sagas of Icelanders: A Selection*. New York: Penguin, 2001.

Weir, Ruth Cromer. *Leif Ericson, Explorer*. New York: Abingdon-Cokesbury Press, 1951.

Wright, Rachel, ed. *The Viking News: Treasure Seekers!* Cambridge: Candlewick Press, 2001.

Picture Credits

Chris Lisle/CORBIS (p. 31).

Roger Midstraum (jacket landscape).

Nasjonalgalleriet, Oslo, Norway/Bridgeman Art
    Library (p. 50).

North Wind Picture Archives (pp. 5, 62, 70).

Pat O'Hara/CORBIS (p. 78).

Greg Probst/CORBIS (p. 56).

Stofnun Árna Magnússonar Ílandi (p. 82).

University of Pennsylvania Library (p. 58).

Viking Navigation (English version) (p. 40).

Viking Ship Museum, Oslo, Norway/Bridgeman Art
    Library (p. 34).

Werner Forman Archive/Art Resource, NY (pp. 27,
    65).

Alison Wright/CORBIS (p. 45).

York Archaeological Trust (p. 74).

INDEX

ABOUT THE AUTHOR

Elizabeth Cody Kimmel is the author of several books for children, including *Balto and the Great Race* and *Ice Story: Shackleton's Lost Expedition,* a Society of Children's Book Writers and Illustrators Golden Kite Honor Book.

Ms. Kimmel became interested in Leif Eriksson while researching the subject of exploration for *Ice Story.* "One of the wonderful things about writing nonfiction is that every book opens the door to two more," she says. She began her research by reading the Vinland Sagas and found that while the sagas provide a framework for Leif's story, they also leave many blanks. "The blanks are what intrigued me," she notes. She set out to fill them in with *Before Columbus: The Leif Eriksson Expedition.*

Ms. Kimmel lives in the Hudson Valley in New York with her husband and daughter.

History through the ages for all ages . . .

Landmark Books® Grades 2 and Up

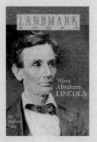

Landmark Books® Grades 4 and Up

Landmark Books® Grades 6 and Up